*Very Authentic Person*
**Kat Sinclair**

Published 2019 by the87press
The 87 Press LTD
87 Stonecot Hill
Sutton
Surrey
SM3 9HJ
www.the87press.com

Very Authentic Person © Kat Sinclair 2019

The moral right of Kat Sinclair has been asserted in accordance with the Copyright, Designs and Patents Act 1988

ISBN: 978-1-9164774-6-9

Design: Stanislava Stoilova [www.sdesign.graphics]

# Contents

| | |
|---|---:|
| Quiscalus | 1 |
| In .avi Format | 2 |
| Oxbow | 4 |
| Pass Embodiment | 5 |
| Situational Dependence | 6 |
| Under the Influencers | 7 |
| Raincheck | 8 |
| Slick Bit | 10 |
| Fourth Stage | 12 |
| Really Listening | 14 |
| Home for Wayward Spiders | 19 |
| For Fiona | 22 |
| Mandated Weather Pattern | 23 |
| Modern Brickwork | 25 |
| Untitled | 26 |
| Down By | 27 |
| ...Hard Enough | 29 |
| Inter | 31 |
| Bombyx mori | 33 |
| On being able to write a poem for David Davis | 35 |
| Two Funerals and A Great Number of Boats | 37 |
| Loose Inhabitation | 39 |
| For Pollination By Moths | 40 |
| Sick Song For New Ergonomics | 42 |
| Licensed Only For Non Commercial Private Exhibition in Homes | 43 |
| Heirlooms | 44 |
| Half-life 22 | 46 |
| Vowel Sounds | 47 |
| [for] my fingers | 49 |
| Body Quadratics | 50 |

| | |
|---|---|
| Hoax Fish | 52 |
| Time After Time by Cyndi Lauper | 53 |
| Untitled | 55 |
| Two Out of Three Ain't a Reasonable Sample Size | 56 |
| Card-carrying | 57 |
| Pithos I | 58 |
| Pithos II | 59 |
| Everything about 'A' and 'B,' nothing about 'A and B' | 60 |
| Look There, Behind You! Oh Wait Sorry I Forgot You Aren't Wearing Your Glasses | 61 |
| Ode to Osmosis | 62 |

*for all my families*

# Quiscalus

Spoke in sandbox time providing colour to idiom
wicking at my cheeks until I too am braided cotton for sale
never burned
together did language laundry clearing out our mouths
this is I am a clunking clothes horse
this time around I'm paying
particular attention to my elbows
think I've probably never seen my outer wrists before
but paying no more attention to that
spot just beneath my shoulder blades
gone sour medusa born backwards,
she looked away and all that turned to stone
so yes I am afraid of my limbing trajectory
though delicate fear as with
what-was-snail-feet on pavements
or a museum of many lasers,
my eyes in the centre on a plinth
watching my body try.

# In .avi Format

In April I brought my favourite childhood toy with me
so I wouldn't have to sleep alone
or without a piece of childhood should the rest evaporate
overnight in a sea of flashing blue or intermittent spikes.
Sometimes I could sway like catkins, riverside
or spin in helicopter-lite, summer snow angel
playing washing machine and over or under or
over it's over please can it be over now
I am back again, it's opposites day and I want to be Lazarus
let down gently, by someone stroking my hand-cut head
slipping me an ice lolly and telling me
I haven't let anyone down
that nobody will mind and everyone cares.
'But this isn't about you' this: slow thing or
confessional poetry this:
ode to the self this: postmodern adaptation reboot revival of
something to keep living every 2AM.
In April the house felt bigger
perhaps they crammed another room in there,
between the bathroom and the kitchen I think
maybe they swapped out one of my lungs
for some extra living space
or a crafts room, or an oversized straitjacket,
defeating the whole point but in some poignant heaviness
see, regardless, I voted today in the local elections,
went postal, went less-than-apeshit didn't even
read the names
I want a big childish pencil and a big childish day
throwing my toys out the car window and wailing
while you double back
like you really did, and like I've taken on

all the stories I coughed up like hairballs covered in glitter
double-jointed and drunk, aren't-I-cute anecdotes
home visits and the countryside idyllic and still too still
asthmatic baby, lost your home, twenty pence,
the long amniocentesis of the new millennium
there is nothing new in me now all that I am growing is
regurgitated and beautiful, internal circulation or
"hold the onions" forever
the end of the season is coming up
I'd spoil it all for you if I could.

# Oxbow

But would it help if I told you I was
very legitimate, meandering nevertheless,
dedicating all my works to the NHS,
and I will be an oxbow, too.

Did they give Lot's Wife a name, retroactively
I just think it's funny that she died looking back at Sodom
like maybe we should circle back around
to the salt part.

Everyone's using the word 'savage' a lot these days
maybe I'm missing something
that's just okay now, and context left like an irrelevant ex
I just think it's unhealthy to never bring him up.

If we would only stop looking back
maybe the female gaze could 'exist', or something like that
but there is so much to look at, so many of us back there
I would retweet them if I could, probably.

I'm trying for a really authentic craning of the neck
something they'll believe in
while I'm still a river
while my caveats still have legs.

# Pass Embodiment

Monotonous wine-glass of complaints about
monotony, self-masturbatory
pouring acknowledgement of doing this myself but having
authority to step outside of the
pixel-lined fishbowl
cliche deriding cliche inescapability inherent
adherence to a doctrine the
culture of counter-culture, once-in-an-epoch
generational theorist of our generation burning
books to avoid reading them
best-sellers recommendation cards shelved
front of shop; King Jameses in the back

a beached faith, bleached semblance of
self dyed in unnatural colours
with the purpose of
drawing attention to the artifice of being at all
tracing fingers spider's web of boycott that balloons
until you sour-taste staring down thirty-one
brands of toothpaste and crossing the street to avoid
your ex the one you knew before
they were famous.

## Situational Dependence

How to come to
terms with the contrived groan of your own
waking-up-in-the-morning habitudes when
you know a TV-city better than your own
cellulite house

wantingly, the construction of a neo-cliché: is it
assimilationism reclamation is it political at all to
have a coke with her, share a bed with her,
is it a part of the paternity test results of history or are we
building it a new backbone and
forcing it to stand

I am not concerned by the
knowing of a television-life-space of a
celluloid New York City
any more than I am sandpaper-aware that I have
lived across from those skyriser smiles
never convinced they are powered by
more than cathodes there
is something piloting my central nervous system
which drives me *gladly beyond* to her
own house.

## Under the Influencers

To think that I still had my nipples pierced
or that I still had the bars I am fairly certain
you can't unpierce nipples
so good luck to the milk ducts and good luck to you
way up there on that
rail replacement to Seven Bridges – *how many????* –
bottle of Hooch rolling down the deck
should've had a parrot on your shoulder then you
really could've kicked off and
nobody would have blamed you in the slightest, my love.
Everyone kept going on about the fucking Squash
it was so fucking tender and I wanted to
reclaim the paper bag
over my head with *no eye holes* and pull you aside
touch your face all over
fifteen kinds of baklava stuck to my fingers in flakes
in the place where I used to buy my Christmas tree
make it so you'd never want to make out
then make us better, braver, like, 'unpierce me here'
pointing to where it hurts then cutting off my finger.
We are at the festival it's so nice to be at the festival
good luck to you good luck touch my face good luck
you are my best friend forever and good luck and
that bra you are wearing matches the wallpaper and
good luck forever we are all slick and lit with
good luck tune in next time good luck.

# Raincheck

Would you like to see inside the secret daytime church of
calling the dog my son
of watering my plants in the sink
of discovering a sink full of soil
of hating the purple Starburst
I have bolted the doors I have run the taps amok
flooded the pews now I'm crouched atop the altar like
something by Kiki Smith and my eyes follow you too
dipping behind the lectern
putting the less famous sibling on hold
before you recruit him for a pyramid scheme
drawing a blank on sense drawing
8-point ley line alignments of pizza restaurants in London
trying to explain what astigmatism is to
you at three in the morning
wishing I were a plate of plexiglass (not for the first time)
wondering what it is to be 'cancelled'
come inside come inside
I've an abundance of things to go back on
forked tongues in the road and burgeoning crows feet
holding grudges when I scrunch up my eyes,
when I'm laughing
or straining my bowels
it's an empowerment lasagne in here
dive right in the water's laced with Kool Aid
laced with 'thoughts on this'
we're occupying Portobello Road next week
fucking with the flower market
autotuning the mysterious screaming orb on my shoulder
which I've stopped editing out of my pictures
because it hasn't yet

said anything too worrying,
even if its presence is a bit obnoxious and
besides it's just
so relatable – the mysterious screaming orb on my shoulder
haven't we all been there, in a way?
You're out from behind the lectern now
making loud postprandial hums, splashing about
in the verbage both of us distorted parallel Liliths
this is my Tuesday fucking best this is my birth certificate
this is my last red Starburst this is my son
this is my least haunted slice
show me the burning coals and I won't run this time
or remember what I was going to say.

## Slick Bit

They call her Thumbelina on account of the fact
she uses her thumbs to send kisses and I think
I'm the only person under thirty in the room
so nobody else is
as embarrassed about this as I am
trying to resist the urge to kiss you right now to tap my
slid my phone under my thigh grimace now
they've moved on to Tom Thumb
I am a floppy disk years old is that spelled
with a k or a c as I sign the consent form for the surgery or
the waiting list
I suppose and the doctor turns to the man next to me and
says "sorry mate"
about my healing vaginal canal.
Will it hurt it will feel like a cat scratching over and over
but I fell asleep last time
woke up with new bones burning so
it's worth it and everyone will think you look
really nice today
writhing sluggish still a bit cling film
foot on the loop pedal mark on the calendar
suggesting a new generation
who never knew a world without the PayPal mafia
or the Müller corner
or highest ever grossing film Avatar (2009)
directed by James Cameron.
Birdlike into the next week
squeezing round the yukka to get down the stairs for
some biannual awards ceremony confessing to
sweet overuse of the word 'honeydew' in poetry
for which we must all be forgiven

father for I have sinned it has been six years since my last
Hay Festival
I was too busy posing naked for the next
theoretical life-drawing
sole representative of my generation told to hold my
phone like the heart of the ocean, gun to my head
some cartoonist beseeching me
to throw it over the side of the hull
while the whales roll their eyes and groan.

# Fourth Stage

All signs point to my having an opinion on accelerationism,
spider-plant tumbling over the ottoman
still no toaster no convinced you stole my dish mat
out there on the ice, or left it damp and
growing in the spaces between the Billy bookcases
drying slower than slippage
like that groundhog dream, again, in case that wasn't clear
from the stuck on the first three beads of my rosary
stuck in the atmosphere circling
Laika, or first conversations with her after she got two
Milky Ways stuck in the Fratton vending machine and I felt
chaotic, titan, shaking the tree for her
toasting over a free t-shirt from a Lord of the Rings themed
drinking game and my first tattoo and my tongue
bit through
on the shoulders of allies
living the same second over and over like an
affectation or a love song

This dream, I suppose it was
I think you were there, Jackie, and this is yours
in earnest bleeps and bloops you didn't
intend for swallowing
or sicking up, here, this spotlight on a horse coming
apart at the seams, pantomime prop but everyone
too overcome to interact
so it sneaks up on you, caviar
nestled in the plastic cafeteria tray
maybe it could've been me, in that back end
while the head won't stop going on about
the people's princess,

sugarcubes, the next Assassin's Creed
but I am not doing justice to the banality of the situation
begging everyone on waking and
online to recognise just how
absurd it is, and by extension
shaving inexplicably like armpits and legs
smooth as a sphinx cat
but the rest that's growth I guess,
George H W in the sanctosphere,
wringing it out

We'll ferment, we'll use garlic paste from the squeezy tube,
we'll practice pet-shaming,
we'll stop trying to be everything to everyone so
much easier than being only a little bit
to someone like deliberately failing music A level
or friend Tetris
caught myself on your Adam's apple the night we broke up
when I stayed round anyway because there was a storm and
my £3 shoes had holes in
told you "your neck is spiky", told you
"I'm tired and I wish I loved you", told you
Elvis did Brexit conducting an appropriative orchestral
pangea from a toilet-shaped crater on the moon
where it's neither big, nor a cow, nor breathing
and we all have our page in the Atlas Obscura
so fuck accelerationism, I guess.

# Really Listening
*for Grandad*

I

Said yes we'll help yes we'll watch as it slips
through lights blink signal drops said
no we're not letting you in this is not for kids
this is for ginger beer this is a larder door
you can have a Choc-Ice but then you have to
make tiny tracks
check in when the whistle blows
we're busy in here doing this and that
scoffing at the old car show wondering
how we'll be ruined –
sorry – *how our fun* will be ruined
we're not there yet
we're only waiting for the quivering doorknob, still
I would go to the car show now
so much I would go to the car show just like
that girl in that thing
though she never made it and I would
carry on collecting First Days
instead I'm late, and in London, or I know I'm in London
except it looks nothing like London it's just that room
in a middle-class person's house
that the kids know not to go in
but you peek through the keyhole and
the carpet's a little fluffier in there
no plinths, though, and what's the point if there's no plinths
so I'm in London, just about,
rolling down the carriage like a lost bottle

late and drenched in numbers
May, I don't know where the parts are now
or what's in the larder
or what to say to you
how to say it
but I'm recalibrating in record time
on the Replacement Service to Luton


II

I guess, we're here now, and we're holding hands
there's a woman drooling on my lap
or, my lap is wet so
*I have been all the places I've been*
mind the woman in my lap
*I have been all the place I've been*
mind the wet patch
*I have been all the place I've been*
mind my temper I will hop up on the luggage rack
just you watch
it's like, we went to the toy shop, and I know how I felt
flipping the model railway upside down
nothing like it was a board game or me, Godzilla
consistently there and not there and really
all this is less about
processes and more about the things doing the processing
but how to articulate that at seventy miles an hour
regardless of metaphor
it would be irresponsible to not return to the i360
in August 2019, and do it all again
I suppose we are speeding peculiar across a calendar
known routes and ready pit stops
wondering whose clumsy lettering on cardboard

whose legs half visible from the outside
whose observations on a notepad
whose changes not made
underfoot like knives or rockets
skittering across the Earth hissing
"language is a virus" in a particularly infectious way
so now we all think it


III

Counting instances of my friends
going places to get to sleep
light with it, lit with it,
Rhiannon on train in middle of night
Rhiannon on plane on her birthday
Rhiannon on skateboard at all girls' skateboarding event
Rhiannon sending me pictures from the zoo
my thumb is perpetually over the lens and
I am murky and loving
I am a request stop the slowing down excites me
so I'll tweet about it later but for now
it will be enough to sit on a bench wrong with you
draw up plans in old lipstick to
make homogeneity history or
make a playlist for a day not like this one
when I went to the travel museum in Swindon
for an entirely different reason
who turned out to be awful too
tinnily enunciated
on the kitchen floor
wheel of brie
wall of glass opposite wall of glass
but I wish I'd seen the steam engines instead

instead here comes the swoletariat
making gains in the gym or showing me the time when I didn't ask
but yes you have a very nice wrist that will be useful come the revolution
perhaps, but
talking with you always felt like
writing a poem for my therapist
something I don't think I'm supposed to do
but often come close to, something
Klein Blue, something caviar
this life's luggage
a perfect replica everything exactly the same
except the padlock is different
it's a look, I guess, like
4am in that convenience store, the one that's been open non-stop since the 90s
feels childlike in there,
Monster Munch and day-old bhajis, a bottle of Yazoo
I'm back making potions melting a pile of Daim bars
chatting with the Uber driver
I'm back in that larder,
you're there too, making tiny tracks


IV

It will be a year, this one,
just like the last but more so
and I'll see you at the end of it, perhaps
well, either way I'll see you at the end of it
all of us laden with ginger beer,
the Cheshire caves,
the difference between stalagmite and stalactite,

a room full of rhymes to help us remember everything
except everything I don't want to tell you
which is so much muttered around the table and guiltily
but you don't need to know that, or if you do
I'll tell you at the old car show
so see you there and happy birthday, for whenever it is
you old Scorpio, you
I am covered in bus stops
friends like capybaras, basking
in debt and debt and debt
but contactless
I miss you
carry on with what you were saying
I'm really listening now.

> Written for Gyan Sharma's exhibition at Asylum Studios,
> March 2019

# Home for Wayward Spiders

'I do, I undo, I redo', Louise Bourgeois

When my mother tried to run a child ran her down
he was my age and I was torn in my affiliation –
of an age when loyalty to my mother was
not a given but a gift
and so I suppose she appreciated it
when I cack-handed cawed for him to go
his mother too and I suppose it was in part because that boy
had held me up against a wall three days prior and told me
"Dyke, you'll never get a boy" but it's easier for her and I
ragged nail still lodged
to think it was because I loved her –
so that's the set up, this burns slow salting snails,
absurd on a wire, drawn up taught like
conducting cattle side to side
and *everyone is tired*
of longstanding things
I am a poorly paced Peter Jackson film and I am sorry,
I'll try to give a rousing speech before the diagnosis,
King on the frontline, something about the sun –
Louise Bourgeois, midwife to the Medicis, did you sew too
and did you think of spiders, impossible bulbous mothers,
I see you in my own cells, I clutch the bars,
I am between your legs
I am a poet, fresh off the Deleuze,
crouched between your legs and thinking
what a mess I'll make of this, and how they'll laugh –
who will run me down, which child,
are they born yet are they named,
when a man cracks out a guitar at a party in 2023

which song will he play and
what colour eyes will they roll and
I suppose it doesn't quite matter
because I am no patron to linear progression
or colonial timekeeping,
heteropatriarchal lineage
or my own pathologised medical potentiality,
and no child of mine will ask me to run with them to school
but still, I am a paralleling machine
almost disappointed when I learned Robert De Niro,
twentieth century abstract expressionist,
was just Robert De Niro's dad,
and not a party trick –
so I wonder, chronic, covered in cable-ties
thinking I too will come in useful one day
honeyed with time and talking points
I almost was an organist, groaning brontosaurus in the mist
like absolutely dying
but the focus of the Q+A section of the conference
was whether or not my name was right and how
nominal predetermined existence
affects collective grief
like a news item: PLUTO EXPLODES, never published
because the lede could not be established without the clear
distinction between not planet and
well, anyway,
my point is I guess my mother fell over
when I was eight, and I've never fallen over myself
without her since
so every falling over is an imitation, or an echo,
or heritage –
and if I were to stop falling over (which is unlikely)
there would be no profile, no breakfast show,
nobody would ask her

'How Do You Feel About Your Daughter's Defiant Lack
Of Falling Over?',
she would not be positioned on a deckchair in profile
in the golden hour
she would not grieve,
I am not lost to some sinister corner of the Internet,
there would be no rising tide of children
refusing to fall over
electing an ever-upright leader
but I would know, and I deserve it more, and so does she,
for what she's lost me to, and how I will rejoin her –
this guilt is not Catholic,
but could be, and from what I've learned
knife edges are non-denominational –
so what the fuck, and I'm so young, and where'd you go
poorly cut avocado,
house I cannot live in,
failing diamond industry,
this guilt is booming, baby-bust economy – ante-sell'em
found myself clam-like, waiting to begin,
wanting to tell my mother that I love her
more than I hated him
but I think I'll wait until I hit the ground.

## For Fiona

History hand-stretched me round without measuring
tilted me sideways and sighed,
said it never suited hats anyway
but I never suited it, and I've been made jaunty
just for the night or whatever a night consists of
when it's pounding coquettish not slumped no arranged
so that even my sluggishness is soluble or
nearly okay turning from names to numbers in a one by one
if you play your noise right

She always did and she made me a star out of old socks we
unravelled on the floor one night
because we needed a project which wasn't us
and couldn't be construed as such
there was a violent tilting almost like a brain
freeze but its eyebrows were good so we complement it
slept with it told it we couldn't wait to
maybe grab a drink with it
someday, next time we're in town, we'll let it know
my name never suited you anyway,
I mean your lips, I think
my mum told me I'm a Winter and you're a desk calendar
but you said it anyway and I arranged myself
so best to hear

In fact I think I tried it too and
hey how have you been and I can't breathe now
maybe I could lend you that book you pretended you'd read
come over I'll core you an apple
you won't have to measure it out I'm
ancient and stretching still.

# Mandated Weather Pattern

Dearly gloved, under the viaduct with bells on
but I've had too much, throat's dry and I can't salivate
no longer sure if I would but I want to cry a bit
stop jealous of the raindrop I've chosen to intimidate
down the window
train pulling away watch until round the corner
crass like a ruined night in because you called me honey.
Two men playing draughts on my back softly softly
wonder who'll win
this one or the other I can feel the cheering
like static I'd like to be invested too
but if I turn my head to look the board
tips I've got an axis to uphold I'm putting up
my guts for reelection don't have much
faith in their incumbency
or the fucking ballot box but I was made
a square peg and there square hole
would let the weather in if I were to roll out the box
entirely, naked, spooning peanut butter out the jar and
touching myself.
Settle down, fingers on lips I would wear my house out
looking like that if I could I would budget maybe
speech therapy so that all my rising intonation
gone and I can't
ask for no tomatoes with my side salad or a ride
or slut on my side in ultraviolet.
Onions left to caramelise got distracted
circling vultures in the catalogue and thinking really hard
about things.
See there's a lot at stake
the stake's not that comfortable

but I cross my legs and if I tilt my head just so
I can see the sea and this is all a holiday and I live here.

## Modern Brickwork

So then, wick-like, the morning and the
quick march of teas along the counter-top, the gracious
gendered apology
turning the spice jars so that the labels line up
wait for you on laundry day, rush of skirts, returning
basket-hipped
scratch of somebody talking about evolutionary biology
paying uh
no attention to personal preference
so then do you stop washing; stale sweat

French press
apple fizz
four mirror hips
fought-battle lips
dipping of a head to the juncture and here is a turning
off-road here is a bridge-burning
here is a basket rolling rimming on the tiles
quick march of knees, a counter-top, a gracious
gendered, rush of skirts kettle boiling
bottle of wine never know the safest colour to bring
"come on in, sorry about the mess."

# Untitled

"The thing is, is that the black frame is less ostentatious
than the gold" but
I was feeling happy that day in my
salmon-sweat dress and the tire swing
didn't seem ostentatious nor did it require
a retrospective mourning frame
but I am at a remove and
we are at a remove and we are at the removal van
now unpacking now catastrophically unpacking
etymology and authenticity and
trust this way up I can't carry it
any other it is too heavy and so are you
did you know the hymen would not have to be
a metaphor for broken things
if we did not let it become one
wheels scuffing the same asphalt like buckled shoes
what's more I read a seventeen year old boy last week
into fucking a peach
but heavily and with great attention paid to the flesh
it was enough to let the pulp be; not see it gridded as
through an application camera
I want to make and make and make without
the requirement for equivalency of exchange in matter
so that the world
gets too full like an ecstatic waterlogged brain.
You told me yesterday
you were ready to pick apart your assets I told you
I was ready to sit in the sun and freeze.

# Down By

Shapeless red sack dress and river
into which my colours ran
last time I ever saw my grandfather
take a cigarette and miss those
collectible cards my whole family cried
save me and Dad who rolled eyes and I
who had just learned
criteria for a proper Gothic Architecture
marvelled at the pointed arches
while the pulpit made culpable the lying dress.

Presupposing a deus ex machina
I continue to run
until the whole body of water is pinkish
neither I nor the dress
have the power to turn it wholly red
I really should be taking my iron supplements –
having learned just last year
I should drink before I'm thirsty
somebody tell me why I should
trust the Please Miss! hands my body raises
Cassandra's twin sister in opposites
it's too late and we never knew.

Here it is possible to
divine the waiting the waxing the origins of
a tabula rasa candle dangled like a carrot
only dripping I am ready for it
to run over to be smoothed like Roman notepaper
a bleached dress in a river running clear again
told to take these ones two days before the bleeding

where I am sat marvelled at same-new-ancient pointed arches like collecting cards.

## ...Hard Enough

As if the cold were something you try on for size
and discard
I've spent today

Sometime in June when I was like,
really super reading *Wise Children*
reading it so much on the platform I missed the third
cancellation I could have
gripped the tannoy like a cat-scruff and stuttered it out
everything I thought about
absent presence and sobriety and the can-can
kicking up in my guts

Summer like Timothy's friend's recipe
calling for binbags of spinach
my time with ageing chefs
grumbling about how much it shrinks into a bowl

A theory of thinking there's a notification
light in my right peripheral
but it's only something to do
with the pint glass of water and
these glasses I didn't think to pay for antiglare
I make the same mistake again
then turn my phone face down and make it some more

Waiting for the train to pull away
again (and now I realise I've conflated
two summers and it wasn't *Wise Children* after all I was
reading into things too much
instead) a lady gave me her card and told me to put

more positive vibes into the universe
and to give her a call sometime
I think it was a serif font I think
**HOLISTIC BEAUTY HEALER**

On the Internet miming data for membership
thinkpieceing together
How I Feel About The Structuralist Or Individualist
Narratives Of The Current Climate:
Sexual Abuse Allegations And Not Being Seventeen
Anymore, A Retrospective
so suddenly I'm cold again and the woman on the train
grows cartoonish and cruel
as if you can heal beauty,
or shrink it into a bowl, and splice it with a fork.

# Inter

There were, in fact, mushrooms growing in the
whatever-you-might-call-a-wasteland-but-in-miniature-but-
like-outside-your-front-door,
just to the left of the paving stones and I told her
it was muggy but she said to wear a jumper
you never know and I made you
examine the back of my neck today like, gestured with
expectation and it stuck.

See there are people I love in this room and some of them
share things like clothes and
jokes and jokes which are clothes or the other thing
See there are people I love
in this room with whom I share things
See there are poems in this room
containing jokes (or clothes) and
when the venn diagrams don't align
like two moons equidistant on opposite
halved lemonworlds I wonder

but I wasn't there for half the references and still
I love them fondly because
they happened and they happened
to people I love in this room and some of them share
things like memories I don't have
but they do and I laugh anyway.

So when I'm talking, wearing my Woman on my sleeve,
about accessibility I mean –
nevermind. I mean that joy is accessible if,
offered rare, in the kitchen for minutes only

like when all you can bring yourself
to cook is pasta, in minutes, in dressing gowns, intimately,
to be eaten back in bed and wasn't that an
exaltation I seem incapable of
calling anything by its name except in Catholic

like most days I am wittier than you
in the most tender way I mean
there are women coming into the shop
for their girlfriends knowing
she prefers a plainer sock and coffee black two sugars
or peppermint on anxiety days and on days
when you have taken modafinil I can tell because you get to
the pun before I do and I feel like fifty
tiny knowing fists or paws.

About accessibility and
venn diagrams and sex pasta sex God I
couldn't stop to look at the mushrooms
because I was tensing my bladder
that's what trying is, a swollen misjudged organ,
and sometimes I feel like *Maman* (Bourgeois, 1999)
and sometimes I feel like the space between her legs,
all of them.

# Bombyx mori

When I was a young catechism
and oh, last week debating the
political ramifications of the word
over broken glass and barbequed antifa sensibilities
arse first into the breach
he said she was a whiner and that all things are stratified
along a railway track we are tied to
in no particular order
but then who are the figures
wandering the lines and inspecting
poking with sticks and choking on train fare?

I used to struggle against
my railway bonds but the man next to me
told me it was useless unless we all did it at the same time
boy, and it was so *fucking hard*
to get everyone to lift up at once –
this did not calm me but I noticed his wrists
were wrapped in paper
where mine were fine silk,
slept like a third rail.

If you ask him does this not remind you of an old movie
are we not damsels in distress
he tells you there are no damsels in class war.

So then, Oxfam in Haiti,
restoring Grimes to a factory setting,
all this wedding like a greenhouse
we renationalise the railways,
a whole nation on track to itself

who cares who you're lying next to
when it's all one big bed, the antifascist bed and
shut up and relax your wrists and maybe
some of us are rutting
up against our bonds and maybe
some of us are cowed into submission
but listen, there's a train coming
so why should I care?

I think you get up in the middle of the night, sometimes,
pockets full of paper –
these figures are body-doubles,
you need to stretch your legs,
wandering the lines, poking the man who took your place.

I think something like that but it's probably
too specific, too tied to another place on the track,
this paper looks like silk
from far away and the big picture is really fucking big.

                Written for the Sussex Strike zine, March 2018

## On being able to write a poem for David Davis

David Davis I would like to be able to write a poem for you
I would like to be able to write a poem for you
if only Francesca Woodman were not so in my head
if only I weren't so much thinking
about how well you are doing
and not who you are
or how you are, or who the fuck do you *think* you are
I just don't have the time to write a poem for you
what with all this space taken up by Francesca Woodman
who just won't go away, or will, and that's the problem:
how can you be so much a ghost,
so much not there, that you stick?
How can you be so much doing nothing and still
do so much damage
it's not a staying neutral, it's not a situations-of, it's a real
effort, I imagine, it takes a real effort –
and that's what makes it so sad,
for Francesca I mean, not for you, David Davis,
about whom I am writing
this poem. *House #3, Providence, Rhode Island*, I think
is what I'm thinking of.
Foot through a shoe through a window
collected now, curated now I suppose,
somewhere (I know exactly where
it is curated I am pretending otherwise
for the sake of this poem
it would be gauche to know too much)
there is an organ playing
or organs. How does one haunt and
how do you? Oh, David Davis I wish I could
continue but I am

quite drunk and so very here-not-here I feel
I am getting too personal –
maybe I could continue in assuming
Francesca Woodman knew
or could know or
maybe I am taking liberties and should be instead
not-here-not-here.
This isn't something you've thought about,
perhaps? We are all very noisy ghosts,
and some of us asked for it,
and some of us sit in our empty chairs and blow,
and some of us are hot soup
and some of us miss the bowl when it's gone
and some of us sleep right through it.

## Two Funerals and A Great Number of Boats

It was a scandal she said, the trend,
so I closed
and the scandals found their way in regardless
'til the house was bulging with it,
Baba Yaga on swollen ankles
slumped forwards squawking
Haven't! You! Heard!
the news
they're shutting down Craigslist the personals
are to be yelled at a minimum of eighty-four decibels
continuously until person spotted
finds you or until someone some
passerby is so tired of it all they
don a disguise and pretend to be found
more interminable beginnings like All My Friends
on the 100th anniversary, April 14th, children's
children in their paddle boats,
panning for the gold ghost of her hull
I too have a distinctive fourth funnel
with no use, no smoke, no fire
flat water bottle booklike propped up
against a nightingale the anecdotes
don't sit right
they rub like we did
hearse down the yard my first suit
secondhand and the hymns sifting
old candyfloss carts old candyfloss stuck older more dead
these mobile homes like my parents
introducing each other to their cousin
hurtling down the yard I dropped out
when I couldn't differentiate

between my translation exercises and my sexuality
parts of me brutal-toothed
unconfused because if I let it complicate
well, more power to the book-burnings and
if you don't light the last one you'll never make the papers –
your arrival is a cotton bud,
Alison storming into the church
condemning us to dog murder
surreal down on one knee
twenty WKDs and let's do it all again
the norm, but this time on a boat
ask you what you're doing with the white goods
he's not even cold yet
but his girlfriend tells me I could be a model
my white blood cells already tiny tarted figurines
some kind of Therese Raquin
not gay enough not here enough not her enough
bedazzled but he bit him on the neck
so now, in the yard, and condemned I guess
it's all wax and useless.

## Loose Inhabitation

Not having written in a while the hand pants "it
hurts to make you heard" so in Winter I reduce their hours;
let them sleep in; moisturise and refrain from biting at the
skin around my nailbeds. I wear gloves.

Spirit level barred there is no way of making sure the
total accuracy of wine equality
in the economy of my home
in the company of guests
so here, I hope there is slightly more in this one –
that is a funnel down which I can filter
today's subjunctive mood –
now please tell me about my own day,
I'll tell you how yours is going and we can relinquish
all personal responsibility for how shitty we're feeling
[you know me well enough to put words into
my mouth, for example:] "Today my avoidance of simile
broke down
like I was - a child - bored with myself –
a wind-up toy – so I
stood inanimate without pretence, unwatched, feeling like
feeling like feeling like
it felt honest."

While you're tucking your feet under my legs
to tell me this:
my tongue running the rim of the glass is more intimate
than all September. My morning choked up
in your windpipe is a diary I can't fit underneath my pillow,
your hand is one I can't fit in mine.

# For Pollination By Moths

Chapped I learned that lip balm's only function was the
further dependence on lip balm and slid it out anyway
told myself it was good and
right to write a poem about something
other than the act of writing a poem or what a poem
should and could be and did it anyway
loved and did it anyway
but anyway I mean that it is good to cross things
not know what it is you are crossing
until you've crossed yourself
right to left and damned it all to Hell

haven't we all been there, brittle and twitching
loving some cold thing to the cheek
all of us, the cold thing to the cheek
what's ivory now is squat and poached and chronic
the caustic ticker-tape
Knower Knows Knowthing rings round like
do not cross
crime scene
not heard right but known well
we are experts in the dearth of expertise
we write in about it
we wag our fingers
it is so old here, how did we let it get so old

Slick smile thought think ache read that I should work a day
for real though that I should
step down from the structure that she should
descend with me and pelted in spirals cut my hair

so it wouldn't get caught up in the food prep
so I can't sling it
out the window though plenty of things get slung in
read that I'm out of touch
or have been or will become out of touch that
I have no personal stake in this
and aren't we delighted aren't we
terminally delighted aren't we
bad work and worse, workers

Lord make me slick if I am not beyond repair
I'd like to be a hockey puck at least before I go
slide me out of your pocket touch no more lips
in sins of fraud and violence and treachery
in sins of incontinence we find ourselves
in parallel triangles in dire straits in German and Italian
in base and Higher Hells
across the way there is that thing from which I am
supposed to have stepped down or someone did once
paid to Heritage and viewed its rooms
but it is breathing still and it distracts the viewer
from the grounds which were never well-kept
so do you think it's dry enough to kill to burn
it is so cold here, how did we let it get so cold

So I know every sandwich, what it stood for
all in its constitutive parts and how my still-cracked spine
would correspond I am an expert in my own deconstruction
and so, thank God, are you –
maybe we could redistribute something else, sometime
I mean we did it anyway.

## Sick Song For New Ergonomics

Listen, I learned a new recipe today and have
forgotten all else
even toast even mint. You knocked at something
in my gut like a bloodened funny bone
twinging cotton-strong cut like paper
months preoccupied with
acne on the moon, carrion roadside
how I've never seen a living armadillo
only its shielding, stilled and how I wish I had something
more than skin but I am slipping out again
thanks to the miracle of blocked sunlight,
late for the great work
curtaining up. I've saved a world for you its membranes
brushing thighs with another I think
I'll have to save instead from you.
I learned what friction is today, and carpet,
candling, the colour blue and here, the proper way to hold a
scalpel – woke up this morning with
hands full and thought this is
probably something we should know,
and we're all about honing skills these days.
Forward digging, trying to establish a self-sufficiency
with ragged nails and treason,
we are all gestures and tossing heads,
tripping over the uneven paving stones and pretending
not to be embarrassed,
pretending not to look back.

# Licensed Only For Non Commercial Private Exhibition in Homes

Truer it became, disingenuously
felt until I'd distanced myself
so far back from this body – threadbare patches
thumb-rubbed running over
what once was comfort; sickly pleased that skin
resists the same now it's like stroking a
cat backwards it's like
rubbing your hands the wrong way up your
own thighs in a velvet dress on the other side
of the night –
in backwards stumble
playing grandmother's footsteps
around the world's circumference so
that I bumped into myself and
woke her so she
span round freshly soled to take me in "Oh,
that's where you've been."

# Heirlooms

In time-infested waters of my
great-grandmother's evening dresses
flannel pyjamas my mother's hands on silk wondering
at my own viscose-rips the word *lush* misleading: lips dry
getting worse or getting bitter.
Just so happens that my house is positioned atop a hill
meaning that I can gaze out my window
that there is a view onto which
I can project my desire to look down and feel
idiomatically small
*like ants!*
"Look, there's a whole world out there
subject to the position of your house on this hill."
Walking down to the train station,
six ay em, sea in the distance,
see in the distance a boat
pretend to feel what I assume it is you're supposed to feel
when you see a boat in the distance
on the distant sea
trip on the curb,
stumble for a couple of feet and the sea slips
from view and now I'm not sure of which
emotion to adopt, I tend to go with what's most cinematic –
almost turn and climb
back up the hill complete a three sixty stumble
forge circuitry from my day like the symmetry
of my knuckles crack
setting your teeth on edge meaning you
click your pen which sharpens the knife in my gut it
seems I'm full of these malignant loops.
One tattoo begins to mean something only now

two point five years after its inception
like something you learn to feel or
someone you say you are.
Say I was back in bed under that time-fucked blanket
some hexagons more susceptible than others
pointing to my early fixation with the bubble indicator,
tiny-windowed
neon green and precursor to all desire
for whatever off-kilter doesn't mean
for the blank-space of myself,
not mass but weight-distribution
being the problem; gravity's poking fingers; the
way my sexuality pirouettes on either foot and pretends
for the sake of audition that it does not favour anything.
Subject to the position of my house on this hill
I look down, project.

# Half-life 22

Cataracts scattered about the backs of my eyes, sockets
a gateway to grey matter
threshold criss-crossed with crime scene tape
I feel – I don't feel beyond the slope of my
shoulders the load, knotted and
product of a fall – much at all

(like) taking
a historicist approach to my school days concluding with
a formalist approach to my mental illness

Facing these: anagrammatic organs
can I untangle the origins of lungs before breath
a heart before its beat
skin before desire or
prior to scuffed shoes, carpet burns I have
become something else
fashioned from a language I no longer speak
though in its holy books I still find solace

Something which does not nourish
long shelf life and ionising time to
decompose in the pits of my stomach if I eat
enough of it – swallow chewed gum and words –
until I am filled up will I still be
hungry – is there always space-beyond-space?
We are all of us mostly the vacuum between
nucleus and superposition

There is room.

# Vowel Sounds

Oh but I am alpaca farms at my mum's mum's funeral
who is not my grandmother
wrapped in this gold end-of-the-marathon turkey dress
asleep in all the ways that count
wallabies in the Sussex Downs
are they offended to be made foxes
in a dash by the bins at orangelight
say hello blissful train carriage tickertape
what am I speeding under
what am I saying under whose watchless eye,
yellow under the chin
but telling no playground truths
sick like a bloodsport wrong like a swallowed 'actually'
all day the world all day its curdled in a longread
telling me to sneeze so that I am an aborted attempt
which is sound in itself
but nothing you could compare to orgasm
or a well-stocked fridge
but what did I expect,
they fuck you up, your *come on, man* –
it's not supposed to Flannery like this
there aren't even any peacocks or at the very least
when he stops checking your ticket and moves past
shows you his back the colours stay the same,
okay, so I guess I wasn't anxious about
having my ticket checked
I can at the very least retroactively assume and pat myself
on my peacockless back
it's not supposed to be like my mum's mum's funeral
who is not my grandmother?
Who among us has not been my grandmother

the chorus shifts from foot to foot
itching under their alpaca costumes
she rests her case, it's all she can.

## [for] my fingers

Woodlouse transformation on waking
sudden replagued by facts and frenzies
like needing not to touch the matted dust on the stairs
with footed socks until last Thursday morning
when you knew – or tasted something the shape of knowing
like knowing ran through your skull and
left its cartoonish shape
to let in the breeze and bacteria – that if you didn't
scrape the once skin from the carpet by hand
there would be no waking up a woodlouse
let alone an uncurling.
What's more grotesque is the whistling;
What's most at stake is cuticle care. The way cliffs feel
intimate now because
you read in some waiting room somewhere
that climax is supposed to feel like that,
a tipping. You wonder if you should avoid the beach –
or sex. Something has to be done about the thrumming.

## Body Quadratics

Sleeping in but waking into an immediate set of equations
in need of balancing before I start on
figuring out the half life of each bath bomb
so that I might take infinite baths and
never have smooth fingers again
but I'm losing all my patience for metaphor
I only mean to say that I'll miss you
that this is not like loss, only loss is,
but I think I'll break poetry –
steeping feelings like tea
like mathematics like figuring out the
marginal utility of my emotions
like how many muscles in a smile
how many muscles in a frown
how many muscles I want to use today, in total and just
go from there.

Starting off by
recycling batteries at the battery recycling point
at the supermarket where I can do absolutely everything
here, let me do absolutely everything and then I'll be
jumping on the back of a trolley and
careering off the pavement
off a career offside going off going off on one
my fridge is empty or, my fridge is full but it's so empty
going full metaphor ahead again I'll text you instead:
"we are all just rain on a glass roof and we are all just
trying to get to sleep under the sound of ourselves"
but you respond with a camel emoji and I know
exactly what you mean.

Can we queer the structure of the house please
I want to be a door and ajar both at once
more than the sum of my parts but less than six
and smaller than a toaster if we're playing that game
see, I think we are: 'animal vegetable mineral'
coffee shop, corner shop, campus shop
bath bomb, half a bath bomb, half of that bath bomb
taking my trolley off road and trying to look slick about it
trying to just *be* my groceries today so
could you tick me off the list, could you tuck me in
balance this last one for me
spread yourself out on the sheets and remember to save.

# Hoax Fish

Take this, you bishop fish you sea monk,
a morning sip of liquid concrete
to replenish what solidified and crumbled overnight
in the sixteenth century we would have gone
down in history
but we've all been done before, by now
which is okay, I think I would rather be nodal than not
we are all significant, after all
even as we sit atop each other so that thigh over cheek over
gum disease, inherited, not developed,
I am always sure to say
when I am next to somebody at the sink for the first time
flecking them sweetly
or, I am not just a tongue, comically large statement
this really is my whole body, the shell is misleading
for my next birthday all I want is for God to give me the
silent treatment
I think I've been lavished with enough significance now
besides I'm not *like* other girls,
but I can't just be a pillar of salt –
they don't make them like that anymore
because here, let me sit with you, clinking cup to cup
we are swallowing seeds here with the concrete
and no longer distinguishing the dandelions from the rest.

# Time After Time by Cyndi Lauper

Starting out this summer fumbling the ball
bursting the bubble keeping us all under wraps
trawling wikiHow for the most
pleasing facial arrangements
sliding my nose slightly to the left so as not to offend
a tweak of the lips, like lilies, not appropriate for a wedding

Saw one of my tweets stolen snuck tucked into a poem
or didn't see it but N told me she'd seen it or heard it
so here I have stolen snuck her experience too and
think to tweet about what happened would be to imply
that I have made tweets worth stealing
which would set me up
for scrutiny and
expectation and
maybe he did just have that thought, too,
it's not a very good one
so I'll let him have it
because it's no fun to write poetry about startups and
I'm stuck on much else to think about
even my bee box has become a coworking space
I want to drag the corners of my own life
into the right hand half of the screen
so I can busy myself with the Pacman ghosts on the left
and never have to know you again

But I'm really getting there with the rainbow paintbrush
this meritocratic omelette, all the good names being taken
when all of our pets have pets
you should know I've got caps in all the wrong places
or, I'm thinking of getting really into serif this year

just like, medicinally, so
someone said it helps with your cortisol, or night sweats
on the long Green Park change

At the climax of the movie when the two girls are wearing
matching dresses in three shades of gauche and
the 1980s kicks in it's every day shuffling
in a circle on our blocky heels
and my pager goes off to tell me
someone's plagiarised someone again
we've all got to be on the lookout
they're after our intellectual property
wait to be told which neighbourhoods are dangerous
digital chastity belt over digital pockets
to keep hold of all this virtual thinking I'm doing
before it's too late
out there on the black market
all those thoughts about the commons I haven't had yet
while the shop that shut down
years ago keeps sending me emails
we all mourned the death of the high street but it greets me,
ghoulish, offers me ghost sweets
"Pick and mix, bitch"
so I do, or something like that.

    Written for Brandon Brown and 'Panda's Friend', 2019

# Untitled

Silverfish,
in the sink at work
close to sick up in my not-my wine glass
barely washed and I will barely wash
but curious
up the megapixels I want to examine
how you work why you are holed up in the staff room
while there's a whole library out there
five floors, though the lift's a bit temperamental
and you are very small
vigilant, silverfish, I won't tell anyone
you've been in here all night maybe we could
meet back here tomorrow, talk about, well
we can't unionise, exactly
I am outsourced and you are very small
but stay out of my not-my wine glass
alien, sheen, sort of like a
it's radical how you are in the sink
it's radical how I am swilling
there is no water cooler, there is nobody
watching it is ten past ten
seven pounds and eighty three pence
five floors
thirty-six megapixels and you are very small.

# Two Out of Three Ain't a Reasonable Sample Size

Life continues to be the Monty Hall problem
probabilities all over the shop,
and if I pick this hand to hold
what's the likelihood of that other
hand over there pulling me sideways
to another circle of Hell, the one we can't talk about
anymore because it's all so bloody PC
told them don't call me that told them
call me *this* Kathleen told me
"your doctors appointments must be fun"
when they only gave me
two co codamol and a biscuit after knife-camera
"just cleaning up in here"
wanting to, I am not a *kitchen* hearing
"I don't think she's going to be *okay*"
feeling alienated from the institution
but not alienated from the alienation *from* the institution
because that is where I have levelled my community
dug it up excavated it from around the uterus
smaller than I'd thought deeper than I'd hoped
mate I'm telling you if the soil was richer-
anyway all of this is syllogism
it's a false projection of the commons onto a rough wrought
piece of papyrus
I did not consent to my skin
being turned overleaf but here we are
on the stretcher all of us except you put yourself here
voluntarily you are attached to it
would be a sign of weakness to unhook yourself now
there is one glass only and it is forty-nine percent full
and it is an antique and it would be a travesty to fill it.

# Card-carrying

My mother, the opera, my therapist
I miss them, I asked my dad why she was dying there
in the stage gutter and
he didn't laugh he took it seriously as well he should have
much as he did when I made my demands:
a lava lamp; a beaded curtain; a disco ball
so my pockets were lined with the seventies
I was always a little in love with the paunch of the world
like tiny communisms
since we can't build them big these days our architecture's
all accommodating
only little barricades will do
like, I could not have been a nun but
I could have made the vows
I'd line the chairs up in rows and break them,
call it useful, leave them there
a monument to incapacity,
nostalgic inability to adapt to the local culture
liberté, égalité, matinée
and I know that I am a good poet
and I do not know that I am good
it's like, I want to tell everyone I'm speaking to and
haven't seen in a while
that I'm going through
a period of profound *change* right now and could they
bear with me but they only asked me how my day has been
I have to text my mother
during poetry readings these days and look
rude and young and capital
really it's Kony 2019 we're
really gonna stop him this time lads.

## Pithos I

Pinch by pinch
you find the freshwater
in the wringing of your soul
squeeze out the salt, collate,
apply to your cosmetic wounds,
leave the bleeding inside
to a fate which stings less in the moment
where there is risk of infection
but no immediate distress

Appeal to histrionics; truths:
you like the dull ache
you wish it would linger
like ringing in your ears

You like a prickly cover, cactus-spined,
wrapped around your latches
better than an easy flick of the clasp (if
you even had one), the
breaking of an equal chance the –
one point nought – probability
of there being nothing there to fix
or float away.

# Pithos II

Repetition as stupefaction as robotic as
newness as never been done before as the
news as the cycle as the daily
segment as stop nagging me as ball and
chain as toilet seat up as fable as boy who cried infinitive

confidence (shaken) stirred not
laicite groupthink hysterics woman time of the month
wolf howling at the moon
woman howling at the campaign for nuclear disarmament
irrational three days of highest *what's your MBTI
type* concentration hormonal

concentration concentrate – healthier than the old stuff
drink it straight from the carton
no need to use a glass
no need to look through a glass (when is a ceiling
not a ceiling when it is a floor)

to see dominion everywhere: testoterogeneous isotrope
to never know and never stop
to scream.

# Everything about 'A' and 'B,' nothing about 'A and B'

Conceptualising the body as a series of scattered images
disembodiment of a blood pressure
depersonalisation of a sex life
dissociation of a one night stand with an ex
forgetting whether or not you
bought the two pints in your left hand
contextlessness of a dating history
expressed as a series of ones and noughts
(a catalogue of wons and nots)

each beast a tangled-headphones knot a – Shakespearean –
nouveau-neo-copy-plagiarised Cicada 3301
setting and solving the puzzles,
disappearance over the threshold
small following,
*une touche de thé*,
there is a limit on how many
unique hits such a page can accumulate before
a 404 such a limit has not yet been hit but I expect in
daily self-examination – puckering or dimpling,
thickening or bumpy – to know
when the hosting server cannot give more than a
reason phrase.

## Look There, Behind You! Oh Wait Sorry I Forgot You Aren't Wearing Your Glasses.

Quivering spider on a single strand I know
with the tensile strength of a tugging
rope in the insect Olympics
were I to try quivering from it myself –
like from the ceiling and
swing across my bedroom as I set myself up to believe
was possible – it would come away spider and all.
This is what absolute *days* feel like,
mirror speaking after the fact
after the phone runs out or what runs through it –
don't have my own rope in relative size so I settle
for quivering here on the bus
I know you don't catch but wish you
parallel-would that there across the aisle we could both be
for three stops the ceiling and the spider to each other,
a nuisance hanging before the swipe.

## Ode To Osmosis

Deciding I could play the tuba so just
turning up and breathing in and that's how it all is now
every day a youth orchestra and
every send and receive a new tuba
different tuning, same crush on the back of someone's head
I think I'm only just learning how to do 'summer'
but they're bad now, there's too much of them,
so I tamp it down
like, how do you cross the 3 month minefield of an
environmentalist with SAD?
It's fine, anyway,
I'm a clump of hair brushed from the temple
an unidentified fucking object
navigating the medical snake eating its own corridor tail
thanking God I wasn't born here
only everyone I know.

All the waving hands in the oubliette
clutching at my thighs like they just don't care
don't knock, mum, I'm mid-evolution flashing my ankles as
I crawl out of the sea and
grow legs before launching a new
federal dominance of local television
it's just that everything *seeps* and I'm paying close attention
to the warnings
in every disaster movie but the asteroid is
taking so long to hit
like we're a GCSE potato and everything else is water
but nobody will be around to weigh us when it's done
or measure the strength of the metaphor.

My leg muscles ache now, more aware
of my laughter lines which are just beginning
from a smile which has just ended
reading the Song of Songs and thinking the Bible is a bit like
a Hitachi magic wand
with uses beyond its marketing
like, explicitly, it should never be read with clothes on
or we should all be making notes in the margins
thou shalt ankle boot tan lines
thou shalt huge identity crisis
thou shalt wondering when the Oyster card went defunct
mourning conversations with American tourists
that will never happen again:
"Here, take this, it's useless to me. I am going home now."
I think that's what happens to time
in the absence of proper meals
trying to eat a bowl of cereal
when we got back from the hospital at
half past three in the morning
as if I could will the school run back again.

Now it's all how to write about cancer
without slipping into a series of
cancer is like an advert for women's shaving products
where all the hair is already never there
cancer is like Milo Yiannopoulos self-publishing
a book of poetry full of plagiarised Tori Amos lyrics
cancer is like but look, over there: the vegans who eat honey
are engaged in a fight to the death
with the vegans who don't eat honey
cancer is like I don't have it, and why am I writing this, and
why am I ever writing anything else
a regular Desmoulins but the lantern is a

spot on my forehead waiting to be popped.

You just *get used to it* the laminated calling cards
your new library
your old medicine cabinet, full
your new medicine cabinet, which was a kitchen
your new theatre mask, open in a silent scream
with bolts on, and his name, part of your name,
same shaped eye-holes
you just get used to looking through them and the
self immolation the
cans of worms
or the Duolingo owl, who is capitalism
perfectly distilled and stupid
counting globules of care into tiny jewellery bags and
pulling the strings tight
to be opened when *most needed*,
which is always, which is never
so the globules grow stale.

I just never thought you'd be another ghost on the Internet
like 'Glioman', pun thief, with one introductory post and
we don't know if he's lazy, or tired, or dead
like here it is, collapsing at the end of a trial:
caesura the means of production.

Kat Sinclair is a doctoral student at the University of Sussex, researching the political economy of feminised robots. She is the author of *The Very Real Prospect* (Face Press and Earthbound Press, 2019) and a number of poorly stapled pamphlets printed in her bedroom. She is also a member of the Devil's Dyke Network, a queer feminist arts collective in Brighton.